The Official

IRB RUGBY
WORLD CUP
2015

FACT FILE

CONTENTS

NOTE TO READER: The facts and records in this book are accurate as of March 1, 2015.

Welcome to Rugby World Cup 2015

Rugby World Cup 2015 will be a global celebration of the glorious game of rugby union. Over 44 days, 48 matches will be held at 12 different stadiums across England and at the Millennium Stadium in Cardiff, Wales. The 20 best national teams from all over the globe will compete to determine who can call themselves world champions for the next four years. The Tournament opens with the hosts, England, taking on the Flying Fijians at Twickenham on September 18 and climaxes with the Final on October 31. The Rugby World Cup winners will lift the Webb Ellis Cup, the sport's ultimate prize.

England's Tom Croft leaps high in the lineout v Scotland at Rugby World Cup 2011. England won their Pool B match 16-12.

Richie McCaw lifts the trophy as New Zealand are crowned champions at Rugby World Cup 2011.

The Webb Ellis Cup was actually made in 1906, 81 years before the first Rugby World Cup was held, by Garrards of London. A second, replica trophy was made in 1986. Prior to the start of the 2015 Tournament, the trophy went on a worldwide tour across five continents from the African island of Madagascar to Montevideo, Uruguay.

The International Rugby Football Board
The Webb Ellis Cup

1987 NEW ZEALAND   2011 NEW ZEALAND
1991 AUSTRALIA
1995 SOUTH AFRICA
1999 AUSTRALIA
2003 ENGLAND
2007 SOUTH AFRICA

England 2015 is the eighth Rugby World Cup. Approximately 604,000 people attended the first, jointly hosted by Australia and New Zealand in 1987. Numbers have boomed since then with over 2.2 million fans enjoying live action during the 2007 Tournament and a global television audience for Rugby World Cup 2011 of 3.9 billion people. An expected 500,000 rugby fans will travel to Britain and 6,000 Rugby World Cup volunteers, known as 'The Pack', will help fans to fully enjoy the Tournament.

On the pitch, if previous Rugby World Cups are any guide, spectators can expect to see some astonishing action, terrific tries and courageous defence as old rivalries are renewed and new ones forged. Fans will experience the absorbing spectacle of the world's best players competing head-to-head, with reputations either enhanced or dented as a result.

Rugby Comes Home

Rugby World Cup 2015 sees the global sport of rugby union return to its roots. According to legend, a pupil at Rugby School broke the rules of football there in 1823 when he picked up the ball and ran with it, pioneering the sport of rugby. The schoolboy was William Webb Ellis and his name is commemorated as the name of the Rugby World Cup Trophy. Whether the tale is true or not, there is no doubt that rugby was born in England and from there has travelled all over the world.

England's first ever international team played Scotland in 1871. The match featured 20 players a side.

SHOPPING LIST

The Tournament organisers have to provide a lot of supplies and equipment such as:

1,400 rugby balls

200 kicking tees

200 tackle bags (above)

20 scrum machines

11km of fibre optic cable

151,000 meals served at team hotels

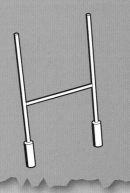

England contested the very first rugby international, against Scotland, in 1871. The match was played in Edinburgh over two 50-minute-long halves and was won by Scotland. England won the return fixture the following year at the Kennington Oval in London. A Home Nations tournament began in 1883 for England, Scotland, Ireland and Wales which would later admit France (1910) and Italy (2000) to become the Six Nations.

A warm rugby welcome is assured to all fans visiting England for Rugby World Cup 2015. The country retains its passion for the sport with many schools playing rugby competitively. Internationals are usually a sell-out whilst the clubs that make up the top leagues tend to be well supported. In 2014, for example, Saracens and Harlequins filled Wembley Stadium with 83,889 spectators for their English Premiership contest. English clubs have also competed with distinction in European cup competitions, providing six Heineken Cup champions as well as ten champions in the European Challenge Cup since it was first held.

FIRST WHISTLE

Every Rugby World Cup begins with the same sound made by the same instrument. Up to RWC 2015 the referee's whistle used to start the opening match was the same one used by Gil Evans in the New Zealand v England Test match in 1905. It is also believed to be the same whistle that was used by Albert E. Freethy when he officiated the final of the 1924 Olympics rugby competition. In this match the United States beat the hosts, France, 17-13 to be crowned the last Olympic champions.

Expect facepaint, flags and plenty of cheering and singing at Rugby World Cup 2015.

TROPHY TOUR

During the first ever Rugby World Cup Trophy Tour, partnered by Land Rover and DHL, the Webb Ellis Cup has travelled to all corners of the world to grow the game and build excitement for RWC 2015. In each of the 15 destinations, Land Rover's *Least Driven Path* has helped take the Trophy to remote communities, and given children at grassroots clubs the chance to see the sport's biggest prize. Land Rover, a Worldwide Partner of RWC 2015, will also be giving children from around the world the chance to be a part of the action at the Tournament, as the team mascots.

The Venues

The 11 cities and 13 venues that will host Rugby World Cup 2015 matches were announced on May 2, 2013. Twelve of the 13 stadiums are spread around various regions of England with the 13th, the Millennium Stadium, located in Cardiff, Wales.

MANCHESTER CITY STADIUM – MANCHESTER
CAPACITY: 47,800

The stadium opened in July 2002 in time to host the 2002 Commonwealth Games' track and field athletics and the Rugby Sevens competition, won by New Zealand. This venue will host the final match of Pool A.

VILLA PARK – BIRMINGHAM
CAPACITY: 42,780

Opened in 1897, Villa Park is a football stadium that is home to Aston Villa football team. Both Australia and South Africa will contest RWC matches at this historic old ground.

ST JAMES' PARK – NEWCASTLE
CAPACITY: 52,400

The biggest sports ground in the north-east, St James' Park was used to host the second ever Rugby League Test match – between England and Australia – in 1909. The stadium is located on the site of a medieval gallows used to execute criminals – hence the name given to one stand, the Gallowgate End.

ELLAND ROAD – LEEDS
CAPACITY: 37,900

The atmospheric stadium, home to Leeds United FC since 1919, has hosted international rugby union before, in 1992, when South Africa toured. It will host two RWC 2015 fixtures with Scotland playing the United States a day after Canada play Italy.

LEICESTER CITY STADIUM – LEICESTER
CAPACITY: 32,300

This stadium, originally associated with football, has seen plenty of rugby action in the past. Argentina will play two of their Pool C matches there, versus Tonga and Namibia, whilst Canada v Romania will complete the fixture line up.

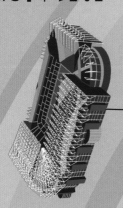

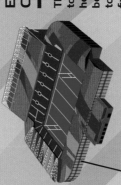

NEWCASTLE

STADIUM MK – MILTON KEYNES CAPACITY: 30,700

Opened by the Queen in 2007, Stadium MK is located in Milton Keynes and hosts MK Dons football matches. In 2008, it featured its first union match as Saracens entertained Bristol in the Premiership whilst Northampton have since used it for Heineken Cup matches.

WEMBLEY STADIUM – LONDON CAPACITY: 90,000

The home of association football had a long redevelopment with the pitch rotated 90 degrees and a new eye-catching 134m-high arch. The 'new' Wembley opened in 2007. Matches here will include New Zealand v Argentina and Ireland v Romania.

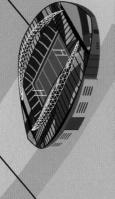

OLYMPIC STADIUM – LONDON CAPACITY: 54,000

Built for the 2012 Summer Olympics, the stadium wowed spectators with its programmable lighting pads on each seat. It's set to host four pool matches including Ireland v Italy and France v Romania as well as the Bronze Final.

KINGSHOLM – GLOUCESTER CAPACITY: 16,500

One of the most famous club grounds in world rugby, Kingsholm first held an international match in 1900, when Wales beat England 13-3. It also hosted New Zealand and USA at RWC 1991. Home to Gloucester Rugby since the late 19th century.

LEEDS
MANCHESTER
LEICESTER
BIRMINGHAM
GLOUCESTER
CARDIFF
EXETER
MILTON KEYNES
WEMBLEY
TWICKENHAM
STRATFORD
BRIGHTON

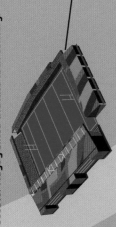

MILLENNIUM STADIUM – CARDIFF CAPACITY: 74,150

Wales' national stadium is the second largest stadium in the world with a fully retractable roof. Completed in time for Rugby World Cup 1999, it hosted seven fixtures including the Final in which Australia defeated France 35-12. This time around it will host eight Rugby World Cup 2015 matches.

SANDY PARK – EXETER CAPACITY: 12,300

The smallest stadium used in Rugby World Cup 2015 will not lack for noise, action or atmosphere. Tonga, Georgia and Italy are amongst the teams that will contest three RWC 2015 matches there.

TWICKENHAM STADIUM – LONDON CAPACITY: 81,600

In 1907, the Rugby Football Union bought land used as a cabbage patch for £5,500. Two years later, Richmond and Harlequins played the first rugby match at a ground that is now the biggest dedicated rugby stadium in the world. It is a fitting place for the Final, a match it hosted before in 1991.

BRIGHTON COMMUNITY STADIUM – BRIGHTON CAPACITY: 30,750

With its padded seats and attractive curving roofs, this stadium lies just outside of Brighton. Matches between Japan and South Africa and Samoa v USA will be held here.

Rugby World Cup 2015 Draw

On December 3, 2012 the draw for Rugby World Cup 2015 was made in London.

Like the last three Rugby World Cups, the 2015 Tournament will feature 20 teams, hailing from every continent. The teams were placed into five bands, each containing four nations, based on their world ranking or relative strength. Twelve sides were guaranteed entry based on their performances at Rugby World Cup 2011. The twelve consisted of all eight 2011 quarter-finalists as well as Scotland, Italy, Tonga and Samoa, who all finished third in their pools. These teams were placed into three bands based on their World Rugby Rankings. Each band would supply one team to each of the four pools, A-D.

The draw was held two days after England defeated the world champions, New Zealand, with a 38-21 victory at Twickenham. The victory was not enough to alter their banding, which put them with Ireland, Samoa and Argentina in band two. Band three was filled by Wales, Scotland, Tonga and Italy whilst band four and band five would be filled by sides playing regional qualifying competitions.

The Webb Ellis Cup is the most glittering prize in world rugby. Every team dreams of lifting the Trophy as champions.

Japan celebrate qualifying for Rugby World Cup 2015 after beating Hong Kong 49-8.

The draw was made by Richie McCaw, Rugby World Cup 2011-winning captain and three-time World Rugby Player of the Year, England Rugby 2015 Ambassador Maggie Alphonsi, Mayor of London Boris Johnson, Rugby World Cup Limited chairman Bernard Lapasset, and then England Rugby 2015 CEO Debbie Jevans. It produced some intriguing matchups including European foes France, Ireland and Italy drawn together in Pool D and a 'pool of death' (Pool A) with only two from Australia, England, Wales and Fiji capable of qualifying for the quarter-finals.

Richie McCaw takes part in the draw for RWC 2015, picking out teams for the fifth band of the four pools at the Tournament.

It took a total of 203 qualifying matches beginning in March 2012 to determine the final eight places at Rugby World Cup 2015. The final qualifying match was held in Montevideo, Uruguay in October 2014 and saw Uruguay triumph (36-27 – leading to an aggregate score of 57-49) over Russia to become the 20th and last team to join what promises to be quite some party. The teams in each pool will play each other once, with the top two teams in each pool progressing to the quarter-finals and the knockout stage of the Tournament.

POOL A	POOL B	POOL C	POOL D
AUSTRALIA	SOUTH AFRICA	NEW ZEALAND	FRANCE
ENGLAND	SAMOA	ARGENTINA	IRELAND
WALES	SCOTLAND	TONGA	ITALY
FIJI	JAPAN	GEORGIA	CANADA
URUGUAY	USA	NAMIBIA	ROMANIA

Australia
Young guns on the up

Pool A

One of the trio of southern hemisphere heavyweights, Australia have an illustrious history at Rugby World Cup, co-hosting the very first Tournament with New Zealand, hosting the 2003 Tournament by themselves and becoming the first side to win the Trophy twice. Although drawn in a tough pool with England and Wales, and suffering a period of indifferent form, the Wallabies are on the up following a summer 2014 series win over France, the return of key players and the blossoming of young guns including Michael Hooper, the Wallabies' youngest captain for more than 50 years.

FACT FILE

First international match: 1899

National stadium: n/a

Nickname: The Wallabies

World Rugby ranking: 5

Rugby World Cup appearances: 8

Best finish: Champions 1991, 1999

Rugby World Cup matches: 41

Rugby World Cup points: 1,423

Biggest Rugby World Cup win: 142-0 v Namibia

Ones to watch: Michael Hooper, Will Genia, Israel Folau

Coach: Michael Cheika

Super Stat

At RWC 1999, Australia managed to play South Africa, Ireland, France and Wales without conceding a single try.

Versatile back Adam Ashley-Cooper scored five tries at Rugby World Cup 2011. Here, he fends off the All Blacks' Brad Thorn.

RUGBY RIVALRIES

In seven Rugby World Cups, the Wallabies have reached five semi-finals and three Finals. Their fierce rivalry with Bledisloe Cup opponents New Zealand is legendary, and at Rugby World Cup Australia have had the better of the exchanges, beating the All Blacks twice. They have also knocked out South Africa at both the quarter-final and semi-final stages. Australia have only lost more than once to one nation – England, most heartbreakingly in the dying moments of extra time in the 2003 Final, when Jonny Wilkinson's drop goal defeated the reigning champions.

Former Rugby League star Israel Folau is an imposing winger or full back. By the end of 2014 he had scored 17 tries in 29 Tests for Australia.

Michael Hooper makes a thundering charge against New Zealand. The openside flanker became Wallabies captain aged just 22.

England
The Red Rose rising

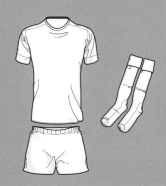

FACT FILE

First international match: 1871

National stadium: Twickenham

Nickname: n/a

World Rugby ranking: 3

Rugby World Cup appearances: 8

Best finish: Champions 2003

Rugby World Cup matches: 40

Rugby World Cup points: 1,246

Biggest Rugby World Cup win: 111-13 v Uruguay

Ones to watch: Courtney Lawes, Manu Tuilagi, Mike Brown

Coach: Stuart Lancaster

Pool A

After a poor RWC 2011, in which England managed two narrow wins against Scotland and Argentina before losing to France in the quarter-finals, change was called for. Stuart Lancaster was appointed head coach in 2012 and later that year served up a performance that England fans could only dream of – a well-deserved 38-21 victory over New Zealand, who had not lost for 20 matches. England's progress has remained steady since and they head towards RWC 2015 with a pack able to compete with the very best, although some questions remain over positions and personnel amongst the backs. With strong home support guaranteed, England will be a major threat if they can overcome the stiff competition in Pool A.

Super Stat
Five players scored two tries each in England's RWC 1999 101-10 victory over Tonga. Two of them, Dan Luger and Will Greenwood, scored tries in England's 111-13 win over Uruguay in 2003 in which Josh Lewsey touched down five times.

England captain Chris Robshaw (centre) is congratulated by head coach Stuart Lancaster (right) after beating New Zealand in 2012.

Martin Johnson, towering lock and England captain at Rugby World Cup 2003, roars as he raises the Webb Ellis Cup.

ENDURING FINALISTS

Martin Johnson's highly-rated England side is remembered for their epic Rugby World Cup 2003-winning triumph – the first by a northern hemisphere side. Victory was secured by Jonny Wilkinson's 100th-minute drop goal. In 2007, a written-off England side managed to achieve something that has eluded rugby giants like New Zealand and South Africa, when they reached their second RWC final in a row and England's third in total.

Super Stat
Jonny Wilkinson is Rugby World Cup's highest total points scorer with 277 points from 19 matches – a total which includes 28 conversions. He has kicked more drop goals (14) than any other player.

Joe Launchbury raises a fist and Dylan Hartley and Mike Brown (right) congratulate Danny Care on scoring a try against Wales in the 2014 Six Nations.

Super Stat
England have beaten three teams at Rugby World Cup three times: France, the United States and Australia.

Wales
Hopes of a nation

Pool A

FACT FILE

First international match: 1881

National stadium: Millennium Stadium, Cardiff

Nickname: The Red Dragons

World Rugby ranking: 6

Rugby World Cup appearances: 8

Best finish: Third, 1987

Rugby World Cup matches: 32

Rugby World Cup points: 919

Biggest Rugby World Cup win: 81-7 v Namibia

Ones to watch: George North, Leigh Halfpenny, Taulupe Faletau

Coach: Warren Gatland

With a very long and proud playing history dating back to the 1850s, there are few more passionate or dedicated rugby nations than Wales. The Red Dragons began their Rugby World Cup journey back in 1987 with a bang, defeating Ireland, England and Australia at the very first Tournament on the way to finishing third. It remains Wales' highest finish despite their 2011 heroics, when they took revenge over Fiji and Samoa for Rugby World Cup defeats. They then beat Ireland in the quarter-finals and lost by an agonising single point against France in the semi-finals.

FIGHTING FIT

The core of the Wales team joined the victorious 2013 British and Irish Lions tour of Australia and are still hopeful of selection for RWC 2015. These include powerhouse winger George North, goal-kicking genius Leigh Halfpenny, the deceptively skilful Jonathan Davies and strong players such as Taulupe Faletau, Dan Lydiate and Alun-Wyn Jones. Welsh fans will hope to take recent victories in the Six Nations and the 2014 Autumn Internationals as encouragement that they can beat England or Australia and reach the quarter-finals.

Super Stat

Rugby World Cup matches have been played in Wales on four occasions – in 1999 as hosts and a further 19 fixtures at the 1991, 2007 and 2015 competitions.

George North swerves to avoid a tackle as Wales play Namibia at RWC 2011. North scored three tries during the Tournament.

Super Stat

Sixteen players have received red cards during Rugby World Cup Tournaments and Wales' Huw Richards was the first in 1987. The second Welsh player to be sent off was Sam Warburton in 2011.

Super Stat

Shane Williams is Wales' leading try scorer at Rugby World Cups with 10 scores followed by Ieuan Evans and Gareth Thomas, both with seven tries each.

Super Stat

Wales racked up 180 points in their four Pool D matches at the 2011 Tournament. Despite sharing 50% possession with Fiji in one match, Wales proved ruthless in both attack and defence, winning 66-0.

Welsh winger Shane Williams dodges Ireland's Gordon D'Arcy during their RWC 2011 quarter-final. Williams is the all-time leading try scorer for Wales.

The Wales team proudly sing their national anthem before a match against Scotland in the 2014 Six Nations.

19

Fiji
Pacific Island entertainers

Pool A

Few nations get more excited about their rugby than Fiji, with around 80,000 registered players – almost 10% of the country's population. The country's successful Sevens history has only occasionally transferred to the Rugby World Cup stage, most notably in 2007 when, following victories over Canada and Japan, Fiji beat Wales 38-34 in an exciting and dramatic contest to reach the quarter-finals for the first time. Two big wins in 2014 over Pacific rivals Cook Islands and Tonga, as well as a 25-14 victory over Italy, see the popular and skilful Fijian side prepare for RWC 2015 in good heart.

FACT FILE

First international match: 1924

National stadium: Fiji National Stadium, Suva

Nickname: The Flying Fijians

World Rugby ranking: 12

Rugby World Cup appearances: 7

Best finish: Quarter-finals, 2007

Rugby World Cup matches: 24

Rugby World Cup points: 538

Biggest Rugby World Cup win: 67-18 v Namibia

Ones to watch: Napolioni Nalaga, Netani Talei, Vereniki Goneva

Coach: John McKee

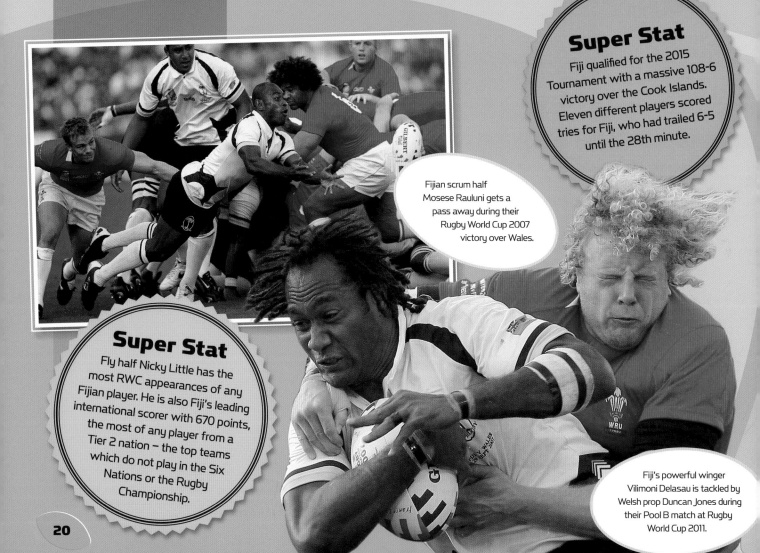

Super Stat

Fiji qualified for the 2015 Tournament with a massive 108-6 victory over the Cook Islands. Eleven different players scored tries for Fiji, who had trailed 6-5 until the 28th minute.

Fijian scrum half Mosese Rauluni gets a pass away during their Rugby World Cup 2007 victory over Wales.

Super Stat

Fly half Nicky Little has the most RWC appearances of any Fijian player. He is also Fiji's leading international scorer with 670 points, the most of any player from a Tier 2 nation – the top teams which do not play in the Six Nations or the Rugby Championship.

Fiji's powerful winger Vilimoni Delasau is tackled by Welsh prop Duncan Jones during their Pool B match at Rugby World Cup 2011.

Uruguay
Thrilled to be here

FACT FILE

First international match: 1948

National stadium: Estadio Charrúa, Montevideo

Nickname: Los Teros

World Rugby ranking: 19

Rugby World Cup appearances: 3

Best finish: 3rd in pool, 1999

Rugby World Cup matches: 7

Rugby World Cup points: 98

Biggest Rugby World Cup win: 27-15 v Spain

Ones to watch: Agustín Ormaechea, Nicolás Klappenbach, Felipe Berchesi

Coach: Pablo Lemoine

Pool A

The 20th and last team to qualify, Uruguay secured their place at Rugby's biggest party with a thrilling second half comeback in their second repechage game against Russia. Lagging 20-12 behind early in the second half, the South Americans rallied in front of 14,000 home fans to win 36-27 on the day and secure a 57-49 aggregate victory. The year 2015 will mark Los Teros' third RWC appearance. On both previous occasions, the spirited South Americans suffered heavy defeats but also managed to register pool victories, over Spain in 1999 and an impressive 24-12 win over Georgia in 2003.

A delighted Uruguay team celebrate after defeating Russia and qualifying for Rugby World Cup 2015.

Super Stat
Uruguayan rugby legend Diego Ormaechea became Rugby World Cup's oldest ever player when he played as a number 8 in a 1999 match versus South Africa, aged 40 years and 26 days old.

South Africa
Boks look to bite back

FACT FILE

First international match: 1891 (as Cape Colony)

National stadium: n/a

Nickname: The Springboks

World Rugby ranking: 2

Rugby World Cup appearances: 6

Best finish: Champions, 1995, 2007

Rugby World Cup matches: 29

Rugby World Cup points: 1009

Biggest Rugby World Cup win: 87-0 v Namibia

Ones to watch: Eben Etzebeth, Handré Pollard, Willie le Roux

Coach: Heyneke Meyer

Pool B

Power, skill and an unrelenting will to win have marked out Springbok sides in the past and the latest incarnation are no different. They are ranked only behind the All Blacks and are a firm favourite to contest the semi-finals. Springbok coach Heyneke Meyer has managed recent personnel changes well, integrating new recruits into a highly experienced line-up. One of the new recruits includes the powerful young lock, Eben Etzebeth, a nominee for World Rugby Player of the Year 2013.

Super Stat
Jannie de Beer's 34-point haul against England in the Springboks' 44-21 RWC 1999 quarter-final victory included an incredible five successful drop goals – a record in international rugby.

Super Stat
The Springbok XV that started the 2011 quarter-final versus Australia boasted 836 caps between them – the most capped line-up in RWC history.

Flying Springboks winger Bryan Habana dives to score a try during South Africa's 87-0 victory over Namibia. It was Habana's 39th try for his country.

IMMEDIATE SUCCESS

After missing the first two Rugby World Cups, South Africa's re-introduction to the world stage couldn't have been tougher, as they faced Australia in the opening match of RWC 1995. Home advantage, a tough pack of forwards and, behind them, the pace of Chester Williams and the unerring boot of Joel Stransky took the Springboks through the Tournament unbeaten to win the Webb Ellis Cup. Twelve years later, they repeated the feat, beating England in both Pool A and the Final, with Bryan Habana's Tournament-topping eight tries a highlight.

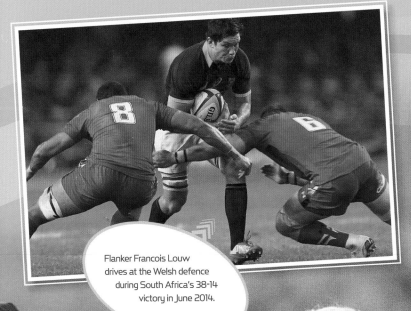

Flanker Francois Louw drives at the Welsh defence during South Africa's 38-14 victory in June 2014.

With Nelson Mandela in attendance (left), Springbok captain Francois Pienaar celebrates winning Rugby World Cup 1995.

Scotland
Dreams of glory

FACT FILE

First international match: 1871

National stadium: Murrayfield

Nickname: n/a

World Rugby ranking: 9

Rugby World Cup appearances: 8

Best finish: Fourth, 1991

Rugby World Cup matches: 33

Rugby World Cup points: 972

Biggest Rugby World Cup win: 89-0 v Côte D'Ivoire

Ones to watch: Stuart Hogg, Richie Gray, David Denton

Coach: Vern Cotter

Pool B

Scotland's proud record of always qualifying out of their pool for the quarter-finals took a knock in 2011 when narrow defeats to Argentina (13-12) and England (16-12) saw them fail to reach the last eight for the first time. Under newly appointed coach Vern Cotter, Scotland toured both South Africa and the Americas in summer 2014, losing to South Africa but defeating the United States, Canada and Argentina in their own back yard. Scotland will be hoping to make the last eight this time round.

Derek White (right) secures the lineout ball during Scotland's Rugby World Cup 1991 match against Ireland. Scotland triumphed 24-15.

Super Stat

Gavin Hastings scored an incredible 44 points in a single RWC match in 1995 against Côte D'Ivoire. In the same Tournament, he kicked a record eight penalties in a match, against Tonga.

SO CLOSE YET SO FAR

Scotland has hosted matches at Rugby World Cups 1991, 1999 and 2007. Most memorable is the first time they hosted the Tournament's matches, when they brushed aside Japan, Zimbabwe, Ireland and Samoa in the quarter-finals, to face England in the semis. Their talismanic goal kicker, Gavin Hastings, squandered an easy kick in front of the posts which would have levelled the scores. However, Hastings remains Scotland's leading and Rugby World Cup's all-time second highest points scorer with 227 points including nine tries.

Jonny Gray slides in to score his first try for Scotland versus Argentina in 2014. His brother, Richie, also scored during an exciting game which Scotland won 41-31.

Chris Paterson fends off a Romanian tackler during their Pool B match at RWC 2011. A formidable kicker, Paterson notched up 809 points in 109 matches for Scotland.

Japan
Leading the Asian challenge

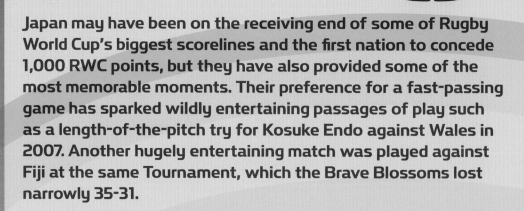

FACT FILE

First international match: 1932

National stadium: Chichibunomiya Rugby Stadium

Nickname: The Brave Blossoms

World Rugby ranking: 11

Rugby World Cup appearances: 8

Best finish: Third in pool, 1991

Rugby World Cup matches: 24

Rugby World Cup points: 428

Biggest Rugby World Cup win: 52-8 v Zimbabwe

Ones to watch: Kenki Fukuoka, Fumiaki Tanaka, Toshiaki Hirose

Coach: Eddie Jones

Pool B

Japan may have been on the receiving end of some of Rugby World Cup's biggest scorelines and the first nation to concede 1,000 RWC points, but they have also provided some of the most memorable moments. Their preference for a fast-passing game has sparked wildly entertaining passages of play such as a length-of-the-pitch try for Kosuke Endo against Wales in 2007. Another hugely entertaining match was played against Fiji at the same Tournament, which the Brave Blossoms lost narrowly 35-31.

Atushi Hiwasa clears the ball from the base of a ruck during Japan's defeat to Tonga at Rugby World Cup 2011.

Livewire scrum half Fumiaki Tanaka makes a pass during Japan's 23-8 victory over Wales in 2013.

Super Stat

Standing just 166cm tall and weighing 72kg, Japan's scrum half Fumiaki Tanaka was the smallest player at RWC 2011. Tanaka plays his club rugby in New Zealand for the Super Rugby side the Highlanders.

CLIMBING THE RANKS

Ranked 20th in the world in 2006, progress has been steady, first under All Black legend John Kirwan and, since 2012, Eddie Jones who has a Japanese mother and who coached Australia to the RWC 2003 Final. Japan won matches against Wales and the Philippines in 2013 and against Italy in 2014. They qualified for RWC 2015 without losing a match in the Asian qualifying process, and are now ranked among the top 12 teams in the world. With players of the calibre of quick scrum half Fumiaki Tanaka, hooker Shota Horie and emerging flanker Hendrik Tui, the Brave Blossoms will be desperate for a victory against at least one of their Pool B rivals to set the stage for Rugby World Cup 2019, which Japan will host.

Takashi Kikutani of Japan lifts lock Shoji Ito into the air as the pair enjoy their win over Wales in June 2013.

Samoa
Tough to tackle

FACT FILE

First international match: 1924

National stadium: Apia Park

Nickname: Manu Samoa

World Rugby ranking: 10

Rugby World Cup appearances: 7

Best finish: Quarter-finals, 1991, 1995

Rugby World Cup matches: 24

Rugby World Cup points: 585

Biggest Rugby World Cup win: 60-13 v Uruguay

Ones to watch: Alesana Tuilagi, Tusi Pisi, George Pisi

Coach: Stephen Betham

Pool B

Manu Samoa are the team no opponent wants to face in their pool due to their bristling physicality and ability to score tries quickly. They made an instant impact at their first Rugby World Cup in 1991, defeating Wales (16-13) and Argentina (35-12) to reach the quarter-finals, a feat they repeated four years later. Another victory over Wales came in 1999 with Samoan greats including Junior Paramore, Trevor Leota and Inga Tuigamala providing the fireworks. In the past four seasons, Scotland, Wales, Australia and Italy (twice) have all fallen to the hard-hitting Samoan side, almost all of whom play their club rugby in Europe or Australasia.

David Lemi breaks through the South African defence at Rugby World Cup 2011. The muscular winger has scored 11 tries for his country.

Super Stat
Samoa's all-time try scorer is Brian Lima with a total of 29 tries. The centre was renowned for his bone-crunching tackles which earned him the nickname 'The Chiropractor'.

Samoan centre Brian Lima attempts to tackle Springbok Jaque Fourie at RWC 2003. Lima was the first player to appear at five Rugby World Cups.

USA
Eagles hoping to fly

Pool B

The Eagles have made it to all Rugby World Cups bar one (1995) and secured their place in the 2015 Tournament by beating Uruguay 59-40 over two playoff matches, with brothers Andrew and Shalom Suniula both scoring tries. USA hope to add to their tally of three RWC victories – two over Japan and the last against Russia (13-6) at the 2011 Tournament. With Test wins over Uruguay and Russia in 2013, their first victory over Canada in five years in 2014 and the sport booming domestically, the Eagles will be seeking improved performances and hoping for a surprise victory in Pool B.

FACT FILE

First international match: 1912

National stadium: n/a

Nickname: The Eagles

World Rugby ranking: 17

Rugby World Cup appearances: 7

Best finish: Third in pool, 1987

Rugby World Cup matches: 21

Rugby World Cup points: 300

Biggest Rugby World Cup win: 39-26 v Japan

Ones to watch: Todd Clever, Scott LaValla, Samu Manoa

Coach: Mike Tolkin

Super Stat
Thretton Palamo became the youngest player in RWC history when he was selected to play wing against South Africa at the 2007 Tournament. He was 19 years, 8 days old.

Speedy US winger Takudzwa Ngwenya is tackled by Italian defenders during their Rugby World Cup 2011 Pool C match.

The USA's Todd Clever looks to hand off Italy's Sergio Parisse during their RWC 2011 Pool C match. The big flanker has scored 11 tries in 63 appearances for the USA.

Super Stat
US centre Juan Grobler was the only player in the entire Rugby World Cup 1999 to score a try against Australia.

New Zealand
The team to beat

Pool C

New Zealand head to Rugby World Cup 2015 as both the defending champions and the number one-ranked nation. The dominant side in the Rugby Championship in 2012 and 2013, New Zealand became the first team since the start of rugby's professional era to go unbeaten in a calendar year (2013). Although enduring a close 2014 series against England, drawing with Australia and losing to South Africa 27-25 in the 2014 Rugby Championship, the All Blacks look on top form for the upcoming Tournament. With the return of fly half Dan Carter and the continuing excellence of players such as Richie McCaw, Cory Jane and Julian Savea among others, this team is looking stronger than ever.

FACT FILE

First international match: 1903

National stadium: n/a

Nickname: The All Blacks

World Rugby ranking: 1

Rugby World Cup appearances: 8

Best finish: Champions, 1987, 2011

Rugby World Cup matches: 43

Rugby World Cup points: 2,012

Biggest Rugby World Cup win: 145-17 v Japan

Ones to watch: Kieran Read, Julian Savea, Dan Carter

Coach: Steve Hansen

Kieran Read surges forward. The powerful number 8 has scored 17 tries for the All Blacks and has been on the winning side in 62 of his 72 appearances.

Super Stat
At the 1995 Tournament, Marc Ellis became the only player to score six tries in a Rugby World Cup match. Eight years earlier, two All Blacks, Craig Green and John Gallagher, scored four tries each against Fiji.

GOING FOR GOLD

After winning the very first Tournament and scoring 298 points in just six matches, it is unbelievable that New Zealand had to wait until 2011 to become champions again. The All Blacks often enter a Rugby World Cup as the world's number one-ranked nation, have yet to lose a pool match and have only once not reached the semi-finals. They have twice been undone by Australia in semi-finals, defeated by South Africa in the 1995 Final and by France in the 1999 semi-final. The All Blacks finally triumphed in 2011, again on home soil as they scored 319 points in seven matches to be crowned champions. Entering the 2015 Tournament, can Steve Hansen's squad win a third time?

Super Stat
New Zealand are the only nation to have scored over 2,000 points at Rugby World Cups, a tally that includes 98 penalties, 8 drop goals and 272 tries, 91 more than the second-placed team, Australia.

Super Stat
At Rugby World Cup 1995, Simon Culhane scored a try and 20 out of his 21 conversion attempts to notch up a record 45 points in a single match, versus Japan. It was his All Blacks' debut!

New Zealand celebrate winning Rugby World Cup for the second time in 2011. The All Blacks have only lost six of their 43 RWC matches.

New Zealand with Richie McCaw (centre) perform their traditional Haka before the Rugby World Cup 2011 Final versus France.

Argentina
Power to the Pumas

Pool C

FACT FILE

First international match: 1910

National stadium: n/a

Nickname: Los Pumas

World Rugby ranking: 8

Rugby World Cup appearances: 8

Best finish: Third, 2007

Rugby World Cup matches: 30

Rugby World Cup points: 742

Biggest Rugby World Cup win: 63-3 v Namibia

Ones to watch: Juan Martín Fernández Lobbe, Marcelo Bosch, Manuel Montero

Coach: Daniel Hourcade

Over the decades, Argentina have been known for powerful packs of forwards behind which a succession of great kickers and playmakers such as Hugo Porta, Gonzalo Quesada and Felipe Contepomi have prospered. Argentina managed an early victory over Italy (25-16) at RWC 1987, but this was their only win in the first three Tournaments. They have since won more matches than they have lost, including twice winning three games in their pool to reach the quarter-finals – in 1999 and 2011. The 2015 Tournament will show if Argentina's steep learning curve playing Australia, New Zealand and South Africa each year in the Rugby Championship is paying off.

The entire Argentinian team celebrate their epic 34-10 victory over France to gain third place at Rugby World Cup 2007. The Pumas scored five tries in a much-deserved victory over the French.

Super Stat
Legendary hooker Mario Ledesma played in 18 RWC matches at four different Tournaments, more than any other Argentinian. In total, he played 84 times for Argentina, his last at RWC 2011.

TOURNAMENT BREAKTHROUGH

Argentina entered Rugby World Cup 2007 frustrated that they couldn't compete in the Six Nations or Tri-Nations (now known as the Rugby Championship since Argentina joined in 2012). They ignited the Tournament by beating the hosts, France, 17-12 in the opening match. The Pumas defeated Georgia, Namibia and Ireland, the latter win helped by three drop goals from Juan Martín Hernández. They went on to defeat Scotland and face eventual champions, South Africa, in the semi-finals. Despite losing that match, Argentina defeated France 34-10 to finish in third place.

Felipe Contepomi puts his poweful right foot to good use during Rugby World Cup 2011.

Super Stat

Gonzalo Quesada may have only played in eight Rugby World Cup matches, but the fly half is Argentina's leading RWC scorer with 135 points. He was the 1999 Tournament's leading scorer with 102 points.

Super Stat

Felipe Contepomi has appeared in more international matches (87) and scored more points (651) than any other Pumas player.

Versatile back Marcelo Bosch is tackled at RWC 2011 by Georgia's Tedo Zibzibadze. Bosch kicked a conversion in the game which Argentina won 25-7.

Georgia
Making an impression

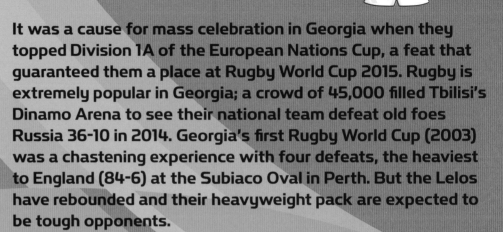

Pool C

It was a cause for mass celebration in Georgia when they topped Division 1A of the European Nations Cup, a feat that guaranteed them a place at Rugby World Cup 2015. Rugby is extremely popular in Georgia; a crowd of 45,000 filled Tbilisi's Dinamo Arena to see their national team defeat old foes Russia 36-10 in 2014. Georgia's first Rugby World Cup (2003) was a chastening experience with four defeats, the heaviest to England (84-6) at the Subiaco Oval in Perth. But the Lelos have rebounded and their heavyweight pack are expected to be tough opponents.

FACT FILE

First international match: 1989

National stadium: n/a

Nickname: The Lelos

World Rugby ranking: 15

Rugby World Cup appearances: 4

Best finish: Fourth in pool, 2007, 2011

Rugby World Cup matches: 12

Rugby World Cup points: 144

Biggest Rugby World Cup win: 30-0 v Namibia

Ones to watch: Mamuka Gorgodze, Konstantine Mikautadze

Coach: Milton Haig

Merab Kvirikashvili attempts a penalty kick versus England at RWC 2011. The talented fly half has scored 63 points at previous Rugby World Cups.

Super Stat

Merab Kvirikashvili is Georgia's all-time leading points scorer with 569 points gathered in 80 matches. The talented fly half has also played for Georgia's national Rugby League and Rugby Sevens teams.

Super Stat

Georgia lost their first match against fierce rivals Russia in 1993. But they have been undefeated ever since, winning 16 and drawing one of the 17 matches played.

The Lelos cannot hide their delight at beating Romania in the European Nations Cup in 2014. This result saw them qualify as Europe 1 for RWC 2015.

A TERRIFIC 2007

The 2007 Tournament will always be remembered by Georgian rugby fans for two great matches. Their team earned a standing ovation from the 33,000 fans inside the Stade Chaban-Delmas for an incredible performance against Ireland. The Lelos' pack was at its ferocious best, stifling Ireland's play and gaining the majority of possession and territory. An inability to convert drop goals and try chances took its toll and Georgia lost 14-10. In their next Rugby World Cup match, the Lelos made amends with their first RWC win, defeating Namibia (30-0). The last try was scored by centre Davit Kacharava only moments before the final whistle.

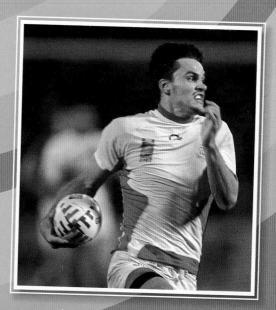

Giorgi Shkinin sprints away with the ball during Georgia's Rugby World Cup 2007 match versus Ireland.

Tonga
Chasing down a big win

FACT FILE

First international match: 1924

National stadium: Teufaiva Sport Stadium

Nickname: 'Ikale Tahi (Sea Eagles)

World Rugby ranking: 13

Rugby World Cup appearances: 7

Best finish: Third in pool, 1999, 2007, 2011

Rugby World Cup matches: 21

Rugby World Cup points: 335

Biggest Rugby World Cup win: 29-11 v Côte D'Ivoire

Ones to watch: Sione Kalamafoni, Nili Latu

Coach: Mana Otai

Pool C

Tonga gave both Rugby World Cup 2007 finalists a fright in their pool matches, losing 35-20 to England but taking South Africa to the wire in a 30-25 thriller which proved one of the matches of the Tournament. The Pacific islanders had to wait until RWC 2011 for a win over a top rugby nation, shocking France with a 19-14 victory and narrowly failing to qualify for the knockout stages. Encouraged by their 2012 victory against Scotland, their first over a major opponent on European soil, Tonga hope that more exciting victories are to come at Rugby World Cup 2015.

Super Stat

With 11 penalties, nine conversions and two tries, Pierre Hola is Tonga's leading Rugby World Cup scorer with 61 points in total.

Tongan scrum half Taniela Moa looks to make a pass as his team take on the All Blacks in Auckland at RWC 2011.

Namibia
African ambitions

FACT FILE

First international match:
1955 (as South West Africa)

National stadium: Hage
Geingob Rugby Stadium

Nickname: The Welwitschias

World Rugby ranking: 22

**Rugby World Cup
appearances:** 5

Best finish: Bottom of pool

Rugby World Cup matches: 15

Rugby World Cup points: 144

Biggest Rugby World Cup win:
None

Ones to watch: Jacques Burger,
Tinus du Plessis

Coach: Danie Vermeulen

Pool C

An 89-10 win over Madagascar in qualifying guaranteed Namibia a place at their fifth Rugby World Cup in a row. Each Tournament so far has seen the African team fail to register a win although they have shown spirited performances, most notably in a hard-fought 32-17 defeat to Ireland at RWC 2007. Captained by the phenomenally hard-tackling Saracens flanker Jacques Burger, and with many on the team playing their club rugby in South Africa and France, Namibia hope to overturn their losing streak at the upcoming Tournament.

Super Stat

Fly half Theuns Kotzé is Namibia's leading Rugby World Cup points scorer at a Tournament with 15 points in two matches at Rugby World Cup 2011.

Jacques Burger drives forward as Namibia play Samoa at RWC 2011. The formidable back row player has scored five tries for his country.

Super Stat

At their debut Rugby World Cup appearance in 1999, Namibia managed to score a try in each of their matches, a feat eight of the Tournament's nations failed to do.

France
Full of surprises

FACT FILE

First international match: 1906

National stadium: Stade de France

Nickname: Les Bleus

World Rugby ranking: 7

Rugby World Cup appearances: 8

Best finish: Runners up 1987, 1999, 2011

Rugby World Cup matches: 43

Rugby World Cup points: 1,354

Biggest Rugby World Cup win: 87-10 v Namibia

Ones to watch: Wesley Fofana, Thierry Dusautoir

Coach: Phillipe Saint-André

Pool D

France are the only side to have reached three Rugby World Cup Finals and not won one, the last being the desperately close 8-7 defeat to New Zealand in 2011. Sometimes thrilling, occasionally infuriating, France have graced many Rugby World Cups with incredible attacking talents including silky centre Philippe Sella and the incomparable Serge Blanco at full back. France endured a poor 2014 Six Nations followed by a series defeat to Australia, but always expect the unexpected from Les Bleus, who will provide stern opposition in Pool D and, potentially, beyond.

Super Stat
Thierry Lacroix is France's Rugby World Cup leading scorer, with 124 points. His tally included four tries, seven conversions and 30 penalties in just nine matches in 1991 and 1995.

Super Stat
Fly half Jean-Marc Doussain became the first player to make a Test debut in a RWC Final when he came on with five minutes to go versus New Zealand in 2011. He was just 20 years, 253 days old.

A dazzling, slick and elusive runner, Wesley Fofana will be hoping to add to his tally of 11 tries.

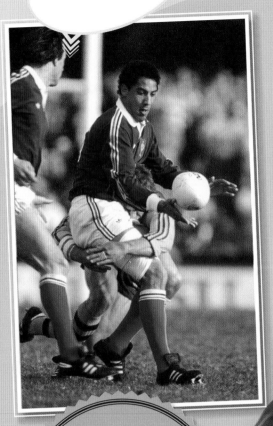

SHOCKS AND COMEBACKS

France have been involved in a number of Rugby World Cup shocks, from a 17-12 defeat to Argentina in the 2007 Tournament opener to their Pool A loss (19-14) to Tonga four years later. They have starred in some epic comebacks as well, the most stirring being in the 1999 semi-final, when they were 24-10 down to the All Blacks yet rallied to score an incredible 33 points in a row to win 43-31. France were New Zealand's nemesis in 2007 too, beating them 20-18 in a tense game at Cardiff's Millennium Stadium.

Super Stat

France have twice scored 13 tries in a RWC match – against Zimbabwe (1987) and Namibia (2007). They share the record for the most penalties kicked in a match – eight versus Ireland in 1995.

With 22 tackles and France's only try of the game, Thierry Dusautoir (on the right) was named RWC 2011 Final man of the match.

39

Italy
Parisse's pack

Pool D

Italy's Rugby World Cup history began with the very first match of the 1987 Tournament when Oscar Collodo became their first scorer, albeit in a heavy defeat to the All Blacks. The Azzurri have won at least one match in six out of seven Rugby World Cups (the exception being 1999) and have won two matches in each of the last three Tournaments. Making the big push to get out of their pool is a priority for Sergio Parisse's side.

FACT FILE

First international match: 1929

National stadium:
Stadio Olimpico, Rome

Nickname: Azzurri

World Rugby ranking: 14

Rugby World Cup appearances: 8

Best finish: Third in pool

Rugby World Cup matches: 24

Rugby World Cup points: 455

Biggest Rugby World Cup win:
53-17 v Russia

Ones to watch: Sergio Parisse, Quintin Geldenhuys

Coach: Jacques Brunel

The Italian forwards scrummage against Ireland during their 36-6 defeat at Rugby World Cup 2011. The Italians finished third in their pool behind Ireland and Australia.

Super Stat
Italy have notched up six yellow cards in the first seven Rugby World Cups and half of these have all gone to the same man – hooker Fabio Ongaro.

Sergio Parisse stays alert at the back of the Italian scrum. Italy's premier player, Parisse has played over 100 times for his country.

RECENT PERFORMANCES

After a winless 2014 Six Nations and a summer tour that brought defeats to Fiji, Samoa and Japan, the Azzurri were in danger of derailing all the progress made in the years before. Previous victories include wins over France and Ireland (both Pool D opponents at RWC 2015) in the Six Nations. Heavily reliant on a boisterous pack led by the world-class number 8, Sergio Parisse, the Italians need to take their own chances and stifle more of their opponents' in order to do well in a tough pool.

Super Stat
Three forwards debuted for Italy in 2001 or 2002 and by September 2014 were all still playing. They are the Azzurri's three most capped players: Sergio Parisse, Martin Castrogiovanni and, with 107 caps, Marco Bortolami.

Super Stat
Diego Domínguez is far and away Italy's leading points scorer both at Rugby World Cups (98) and in all international rugby (983), placing him fifth on the all-time list.

Luke McLean breaks free during Italy's 27-10 victory over the United States at Rugby World Cup 2011. McLean has scored seven tries and 13 penalties for the Azzurri.

Ireland
Taking that extra step

Pool D

FACT FILE

First international match: 1875

National stadium: Aviva Stadium

Nickname: n/a

World Rugby ranking: 4

Rugby World Cup appearances: 8

Best finish: Quarter-finals, 1987, 1991, 1995, 2003, 2011

Rugby World Cup matches: 30

Rugby World Cup points: 819

Biggest Rugby World Cup win: 64-7, v Namibia

Ones to watch: Rob Kearney, Jamie Heaslip, Johnny Sexton, Cian Healy

Coach: Joe Schmidt

In 2014, Ireland gave their world-class centre and leading try scorer, Brian O'Driscoll, the perfect send-off with an away victory in France to win the Six Nations. How the Irish will fare after O'Driscoll's retirement is one of the big questions of the Tournament. In Johnny Sexton, Paul O'Connell, Cian Healy and Rob Kearney amongst others, the Irish have proven match-winners. Yet, despite always possessing world-class players, they have never made it past the quarter-final stages. New coach Joe Schmidt must look to keep his players going from strength to strength to build on their victories over South Africa and Australia in the 2014 November internationals.

Super Stat
Ireland's fly half Ralph Keyes was Rugby World Cup 1991's highest scorer with 68 points in just four matches.

Super Stat
Ireland's squad at Rugby World Cup 2011 had the oldest average age of any team – 29 years and 34 days. It would have been more if John Hayes had made the team.

Ireland celebrate winning the 2014 Six Nations tournament. The year would also end on a high as Ireland recorded victories over both South Africa and Australia.

TACKLING THE WALLABIES

Ireland and Australia are old Rugby World Cup adversaries, having been drawn in the same pool in three of the past four Rugby World Cups and also having met twice at the Tournament knockout stages, in 1987 and 1991. On both occasions Australia won but 1991 was particularly painful as Ireland led until the 79th minute, when Michael Lynagh's try gave Australia a 19-18 win. The Irish also suffered a one point loss against the Wallabies in their 2003 Pool A match. Revenge finally came in 2011 when Johnny Sexton's accurate kicking and a solid performance from the Irish forwards saw them win 15-6 at Eden Park.

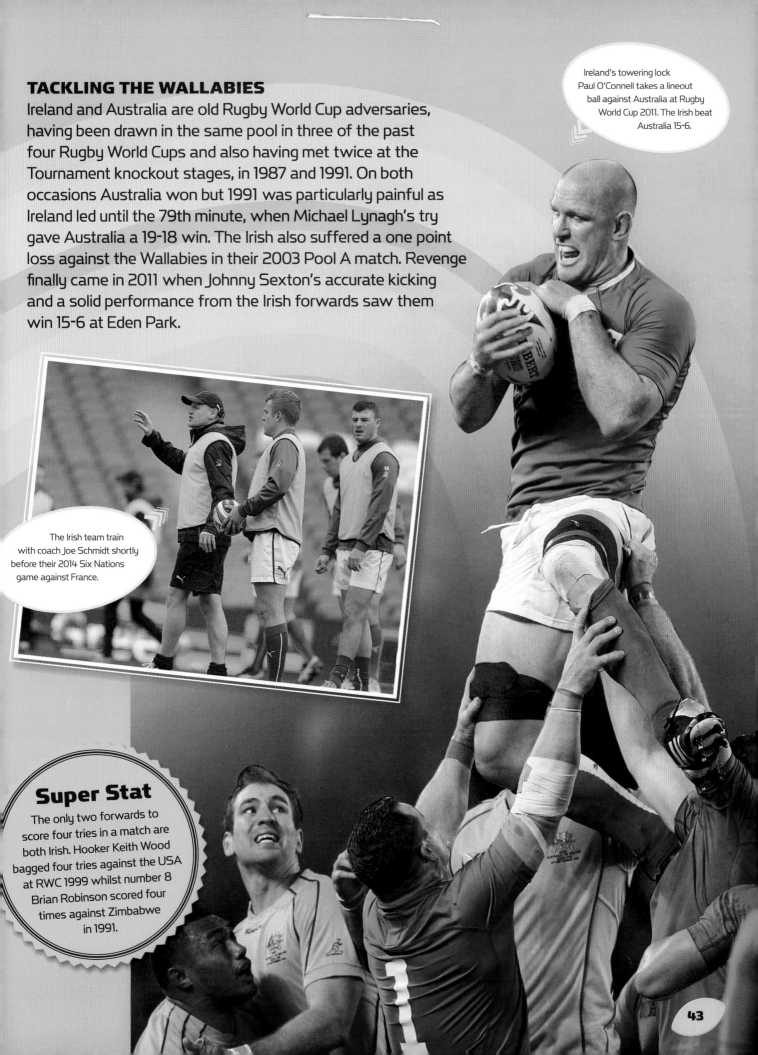

Ireland's towering lock Paul O'Connell takes a lineout ball against Australia at Rugby World Cup 2011. The Irish beat Australia 15-6.

The Irish team train with coach Joe Schmidt shortly before their 2014 Six Nations game against France.

Super Stat
The only two forwards to score four tries in a match are both Irish. Hooker Keith Wood bagged four tries against the USA at RWC 1999 whilst number 8 Brian Robinson scored four times against Zimbabwe in 1991.

Canada
Make way for the Maple Leafs

Pool D

Invited to take part in the first Tournament, Canada have since attended every Rugby World Cup. The Maple Leafs have only once failed to win a match in their pool (in 2007) and are certain to pose stiff resistance, coached by former All Black and RWC 1987 winner, Kieran Crowley. Canada's squad is expected to be a mixture of battle-hardened veterans such as lock Jamie Cudmore and Canada's all-time leading international points scorer, James Pritchard, mixed with young guns including winger Taylor Paris and young captain Tyler Ardron.

FACT FILE

First international match: 1932

National stadium: BMO Field

Nickname: The Maple Leafs, The Canucks

World Rugby ranking: 18

Rugby World Cup appearances: 8

Best finish: Quarter-finals, 1991

Rugby World Cup matches: 25

Rugby World Cup points: 469

Biggest Rugby World Cup win: 72-11 v Namibia

Ones to watch: Jeff Hassler, Tyler Ardron

Coach: Kieran Crowley

The Maple Leafs line up before their Pool A match against Tonga at Rugby World Cup 2011. Canada scored three tries and won 25-20.

Canada's Harry Jones goes for a high ball as USA's Blaine Scully tackles him. Canada won their two matches against USA in 2013, enabling them to qualify for RWC 2015.

Super Stat
Canada have been involved in two of the three drawn matches that have occurred at Rugby World Cups, both against Japan.

Super Stat
Three Canadian players, Dan Baugh in 2011 and Gareth Rees and Rod Snow in 1995, have received red cards, the latter two in the same match against South Africa – the only time this has happened in RWC history.

Romania
The Oaks stand tall

Pool D

FACT FILE

First international match: 1919

National stadium: Stadionul National de Rugby Arcul de Triumf

Nickname: The Oaks

World Rugby ranking: 16

Rugby World Cup appearances: 8

Best finish: Third in pool, 1987, 1991, 1999

Rugby World Cup matches: 24

Rugby World Cup points: 305

Biggest Rugby World Cup win: 37-7 v Namibia

Ones to watch: Florin Vlaicu, Mihai Macovei

Coach: Lynn Howells

Another team who have qualified for every single Rugby World Cup, Romania have been drawn in a tough pool but can call on all-action front row forwards like Mihai Lazãr and Paulicã Ion as well as versatile centre and goalkicker Florin Vlaicu. Along with Georgia, Romania are the strongest European team outside of the Six Nations, with one championship and three runners-up finishes in the last five years of the European Nations Cup. Amongst the Oaks' most notable RWC victories were a hard-fought win over Fiji in 1991 and an epic 1999 contest in which Romania were 12 points behind at half time, but ended up 27-25 winners over the USA.

The Romanians launch a powerful rolling maul during their Rugby World Cup 2011 match versus Scotland.

Romanian centre Romeo Gontineac is tackled by the All Blacks' Sione Lauaki during their Pool C match at RWC 2007.

Super Stat
Romania's coach at RWC 2011, Romeo Gontineac, appeared in four Tournaments for his country as a centre (1995-2007) – a Romanian record total of 14 matches.

Players to Watch: **Backs**

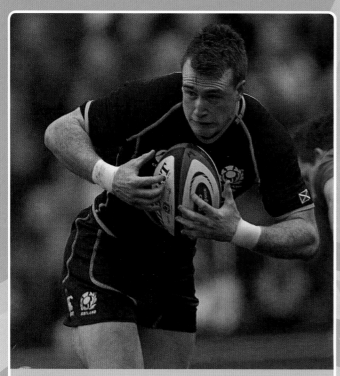

STUART HOGG

Country:	Scotland
Club:	Glasgow Warriors (Scotland)
Position:	Full back
Born:	June 24, 1992
Total Caps:	29
Total Points:	48

Skills and strengths: Fearless when tackling larger players and versatile too, Hogg has played as centre and on the wing but is best known as a full back with extreme pace in his sprinting and cover defence.

Tries and triumphs: Scored his first international tries against France and England and followed up with a 90m try against Italy in the 2013 Six Nations. Was selected for Scotland's rugby sevens squad for the 2014 Commonwealth Games.

Claim to fame: Youngest try scorer for Scotland in 79 years. Youngest player selected for the British & Irish Lions tour of Australia in 2013.

ISRAEL FOLAU

Country:	Australia
Club:	NSW Waratahs (Australia)
Position:	Full back or wing
Born:	April 3, 1989
Total Caps:	29
Total Points:	85

Skills and strengths: The powerful, athletic recruit from rugby league (and Australian Rules) is strong under the high ball, good at dodging tackles and making offloads. He is a regular try scorer for club and country.

Tries and triumphs: Scored two tries on his debut versus the British & Irish Lions in 2013 and scored a record-equalling 10 tries in his first season playing for the Wallabies. Super Rugby 2014 winner with the Waratahs.

Claim to fame: Australian Rugby Union Rookie of the Year in his first season, Folau was also joint top try scorer in the 2014 Super Rugby season with 12 tries.

NOTE TO READER: The caps and points in this book are accurate as of March 1, 2015.

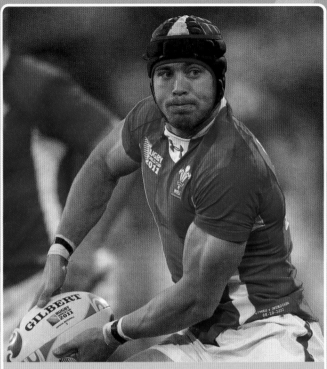

LEIGH HALFPENNY

Country:	Wales
Club:	Toulon (France)
Position:	Full back
Born:	December 22, 1988
Total Caps:	60
Total Points:	495

Skills and strengths: Reliable under the high ball and skilled at perfectly-timed passes. But it is his incredibly accurate goal kicking under pressure and from all parts of the pitch that attracts the most praise.

Tries and triumphs: Scored seven tries in his first six matches for the Cardiff Blues, leading to a call up and debut for the Wales team at the age of 19. Has since scored 12 tries and was an integral part of Wales' two Six Nations Grand Slam-winning sides.

Claim to fame: Player of the 2013 Six Nations, Halfpenny was also awarded player of the series in the 2013 British & Irish Lions tour of Australia. Nominated for World Rugby Player of the Year 2013.

MIKE BROWN

Country:	England
Club:	Harlequins (England)
Position:	Full back
Born:	September 4, 1985
Total Caps:	35
Total Points:	30

Skills and strengths: Feisty and scared of no one, Brown's eye for a gap between opponents and his fast footwork see him frequently beat the first defender and gain a lot of territory for his team. He can play on the wing but is most devastating when positioned at full back.

Tries and triumphs: Scored 11 tries in 21 games as Harlequins won the English Premiership for the first time in 2011/12. Scored his first try for England (v France) in the 2014 Six Nations.

Claim to fame: Brown was awarded Player of the Tournament in the 2014 Six Nations and England's Man of the Series in the 2013 November internationals.

Players to Watch: **Backs**

JULIAN SAVEA

Country:	New Zealand
Club:	Wellington (New Zealand)
Position:	Wing
Born:	August 7, 1990
Total Caps:	33
Total Points:	150

Skills and strengths: Coming from a background in rugby sevens, Savea's quick feet and swift sidestep frequently see him beat his man in one-on-one situations. Big, speedy and always involved in the action, he is a try-scoring natural.

Tries and triumphs: Scored three tries on his Test debut, becoming the only All Black to score a hat-trick of tries against Ireland. Has continued to impress with eight tries against England in just four matches.

Claim to fame: The 2010 IRB Junior Player of the Year, Savea is now a must-pick in the talented All Blacks first XV. He was nominated for World Rugby Player of the Year 2014.

GEORGE NORTH

Country:	Wales
Club:	Northampton Saints (England)
Position:	Wing
Born:	April 13, 1992
Total Caps:	49
Total Points:	105*

Skills and strengths: At 1.93m tall and weighing in around 109kg, North's strength, physique and pace always make him a threat in attack as well as strong in defence.

Tries and triumphs: The youngest player to score two tries on international debut, versus South Africa, at age 18. Has scored 19 tries for Wales so far and there is plenty more to come from this huge talent.

Claim to fame: Won the 2012 and 2013 Six Nations with Wales and scored a memorable try to help the British & Irish Lions win the 2013 series versus Australia. Held the record for most international tries as a teenager.

*10 points from British & Irish Lions tour.

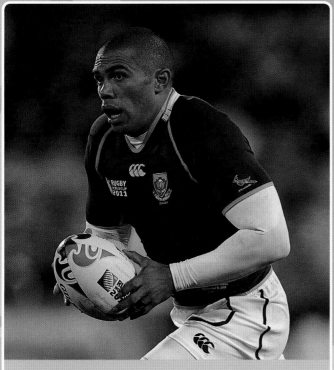

BRYAN HABANA

Country:	South Africa
Club:	Toulon (France)
Position:	Wing
Born:	June 12, 1983
Total Caps:	106
Total Points:	285

Skills and strengths: Hugely experienced yet with a hunger for the challenge, Habana may have lost a little of his lightning pace but remains one of rugby's most lethal finishers.

Tries and triumphs: Scored a try with his first touch of the ball on his debut versus England. With 56 tries for the Springboks, he is far and away the world's leading international try scorer amongst current players.

Claim to fame: Leading try scorer and winner at RWC 2007, Habana also won the Heineken Cup and Top 14 championship with Toulon in 2014. He was named World Rugby Player of the Year in 2007 and South African Player of the Year three times (2005, 2007, 2012).

WESLEY FOFANA

Country:	France
Club:	Clermont Auvergne (France)
Position:	Centre
Born:	January 20, 1988
Total Caps:	32
Total Points:	55

Skills and strengths: A creative inside centre, Fofana is sharp and devastatingly quick. A great eye for a gap is matched by his ability to slip out of tackles.

Tries and triumphs: Won the Top 14 championship with Clermont. Scored a sensational try from inside his own half in April 2013 just 39 seconds after kick off. One of his 11 tries for France so far was a 70m solo effort v England in 2013.

Claim to fame: Scored a try on his debut for France (v Italy) and then scored in each of the next three matches. Nicknamed 'Le Guépard' (The Cheetah) for his blistering pace, he is rated as one of the best centres in the northern hemisphere.

Players to Watch: **Backs**

MANU TUILAGI

Country: England
Club: Leicester Tigers (England)
Position: Centre
Born: May 18, 1991
Total Caps: 26
Total Points: 55

Skills and strengths: The human wrecking ball is capable of running through as well as around defenders. Fearless and with good pace, Tuilagi dodges tackles with ease and is also able to make powerful tackles on opponents.

Tries and triumphs: Scored a try and made two try-scoring passes during England's epic 38-21 win over the All Blacks in 2012. Part of the English Premiership-winning Leicester Tigers team (2012/13).

Claim to fame: England's youngest ever Rugby World Cup player has the ability to change matches and excite crowds with his eye-catching play.

JEAN DE VILLIERS

Country: South Africa
Club: Stormers (South Africa)
Position: Centre
Born: February 24, 1981
Total Caps: 106
Total Points: 135

Skills and strengths: South Africa's captain since 2012 and their most capped centre, de Villiers is a rock solid steadying presence in the Springboks' backline. He can be a bruising tackler but is also an excellent distributor of the ball.

Tries and triumphs: Scored 85 tries for Western Province and 25 for Stormers. Part of South Africa's Rugby World Cup 2007-winning squad, although restricted by injury. His long career includes winning the IRB Under-21 World Championships back in 2002.

Claim to fame: Has been named South African Player of the Year twice (2008, 2013).

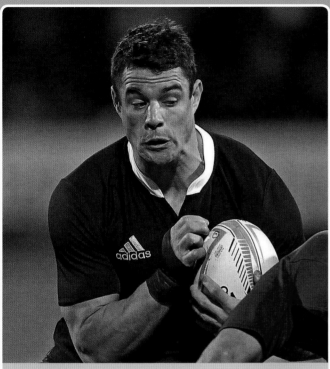

DAN CARTER

Country:	New Zealand
Club:	Canterbury (New Zealand)
Position:	Fly half
Born:	March 5, 1982
Total Caps:	102
Total Points:	1,457

Skills and strengths: Mentally strong with an amazing tactical brain, Carter manages matches brilliantly, can beat opponents with a deceptive sidestep and he kicks and passes with great accuracy.

Tries and triumphs: Picked up 20 points on his All Blacks debut in 2003. Has scored a further 29 tries and is both the international points scorer world record holder and has scored more points in Super Rugby than any other player (1,581).

Claim to fame: The best fly half in world rugby for much of the last decade. Has won Super Rugby four times with the Crusaders. A Rugby World Cup Winner (2011) and twice World Rugby Player of the Year (2005, 2012).

WILL GENIA

Country:	Australia
Club:	Queensland Reds (Australia)
Position:	Scrum half
Born:	January 17, 1988
Total Caps:	58
Total Points:	40

Skills and strengths: Small but strong, a smart decision maker and explosive runner, Genia torments and opens up opposition defences with his quick breaks, sniping runs and incisive passing.

Tries and triumphs: Won the Super Rugby title in 2011, the same year that Australia won the last ever Tri-Nations competition. Has captained Australia on a number of occasions including at RWC 2011.

Claim to fame: Awarded Super Rugby's Player of the Season in both 2011 and 2012, Genia has been widely regarded as the best scrum half in world rugby.

SERGIO PARISSE

Country:	Italy
Club:	Stade Français (France)
Position:	Number 8
Born:	September 12, 1983
Total Caps:	110
Total Points:	68

Skills and strengths: Parisse has the hands and vision of a back with the all-round game of a supreme back row forward. He's equally happy in the lineout as he is making a charge upfield or slipping out an offload in the tackle.

Tries and triumphs: Parisse scored his first try for Italy at RWC 2003 against Canada. In 2007 he won the French Top 14 with Stade Français. Captained Italy at Rugby World Cup 2011.

Claim to fame: Italy's talisman was first capped at just 18 and has led his country to recent Six Nations wins over France and Ireland. Twice nominated for World Rugby Player of the Year.

JUAN MARTÍN FERNÁNDEZ LOBBE

Country:	Argentina
Club:	Toulon (France)
Position:	Flanker or Number 8
Born:	November 19, 1981
Total Caps:	61
Total Points:	30

Skills and strengths: Agile in the air – where he plays a major part in securing ball from restarts and lineouts – Fernández Lobbe is also fearless on the ground, where his expert passing often releases his backs.

Tries and triumphs: In 2006, Fernández Lobbe scored a try in both of Argentina's two victories over Wales and starred in their win over England. He played in every match of Argentina's run to third place at Rugby World Cup 2007.

Claim to fame: He won the English Premiership with Sale (2005/06) and the Heineken Cup twice with Toulon (2012/13, 2013/14). He captained Argentina in their first Rugby Championship in 2012.

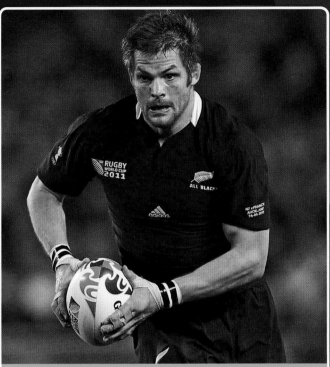

RICHIE
MCCAW

Country:	New Zealand
Club:	Canterbury (New Zealand)
Position:	Flanker
Born:	December 31, 1980
Total Caps:	137
Total Points:	125

Skills and strengths: One of the greatest openside flankers, McCaw reads the game superbly. His strength, quick reactions and handling skills pose severe problems to opponents.

Tries and triumphs: A nine-time Tri-Nations (now the Rugby Championship) winner, McCaw first captained New Zealand in 2004 at the age of 23. He has captained the All Blacks 100 times, more than any other player, and led them to victory at RWC 2011.

Claim to fame: The only three-time winner of the World Rugby Player of the Year award (2006, 2009, 2010). McCaw is the first player in world rugby to be on the winning side in more than 100 Tests.

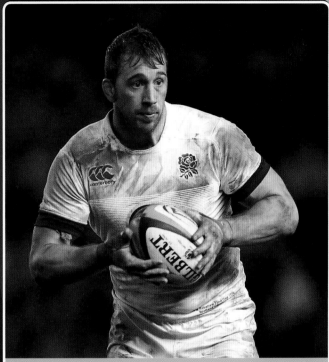

CHRIS
ROBSHAW

Country:	England
Club:	Harlequins (England)
Position:	Flanker
Born:	June 4, 1986
Total Caps:	34
Total Points:	10

Skills and strengths: England's courageous leader is always in the thick of the action. His high tackle rate, strong foraging on the ground and willingness to appear at first receiver often see him top the match stats for carries and collisions.

Tries and triumphs: Scored his first England try in a 20-13 win over Australia in 2013. Made captain of Harlequins in 2010, Robshaw led them to European Challenge Cup glory the following year.

Claim to fame: Twice Premiership Player of the Year (2008/09, 2011/12). Robshaw has played all but two of his England matches as captain. Led England to a 38-21 win over New Zealand in 2012.

Players to Watch: **Forwards**

KIERAN READ

Country: New Zealand
Club: Canterbury (New Zealand)
Position: Number 8
Born: October 26, 1985
Total Caps 72
Total Points: 85

Skills and strengths: A confident lineout target jumper, Read also makes great tackles and carries. His excellent hands, stamina and awareness make him strong in attack.

Tries and triumphs: A Rugby World Cup winner in 2011, Read has only lost eight of his 72 matches with the All Blacks. This included a 14-match winning streak throughout 2013 in which New Zealand won the Rugby Championship for a second year running.

Claim to fame: Captain for Crusaders and twice New Zealand Player of the Year (2010, 2013). Read's all-round excellence saw him crowned the World Rugby Player of the Year in 2013.

COURTNEY LAWES

Country: England
Club: Northampton Saints (England)
Position: Lock
Born: February 23, 1989
Total Caps: 36
Total Points: 0

Skills and strengths: An agile jumper in England's lineout, Lawes is famed for his ultra-aggressive defence, bone-shuddering tackles and frighteningly high work rate all over the pitch.

Tries and triumphs: He debuted for England and was an IRB Junior World Championship finalist, both in 2009. In 2014 Lawes won the English Premiership and European Challenge Cup with Northampton Saints.

Claim to fame: Awarded man of the match for his inspiring performance against Wales in the 2014 Six Nations. He also impressed on England's summer tour of New Zealand in 2014.

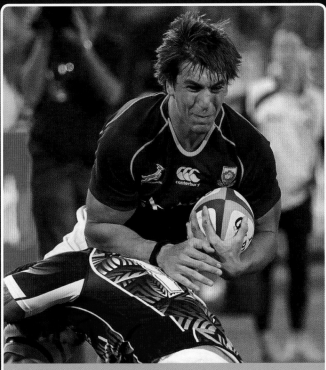

EBEN ETZEBETH

Country:	South Africa
Club:	Stormers (South Africa)
Position:	Lock
Born:	October 29, 1991
Total Caps:	33
Total Points:	0

Skills and strengths: Young, strong and relentless, Etzebeth is the successor to the uncompromising Bakkies Botha. He is a skilled lineout operator and is unstoppable in defence and in driving forward with the ball.

Tries and triumphs: Scored six tries for Western Province with whom he won the Currie Cup in 2012. His driving play has been instrumental in South Africa losing just five out of 26 international matches.

Claim to fame: Was nominated for World Rugby Player of the Year in 2013. Arguably the best young lock in world rugby, the Springboks hope he will continue to go from strength to strength.

PAUL O'CONNELL

Country:	Ireland
Club:	Munster (Ireland)
Position:	Lock
Born:	October 20, 1979
Total Caps:	105
Points:	30

Skills and strengths: Heading towards his fourth Rugby World Cup, the veteran lock remains a terrifying opponent, an inspiring leader and strong in all aspects of forward play. He is especially skilled in both mauls and lineouts.

Tries and triumphs: Scored a try on his Ireland debut (v Wales) in 2002. Won the Six Nations in 2009 and 2014 and two Heineken Cups in 2006 and 2008.

Claim to fame: The long-serving skipper of Ireland is one of the few players to be selected for three British and Irish Lions tours (2005, 2009, 2013). Lions captain in 2009 and a former nominee for the World Rugby Player of the Year.

Players to Watch: **Forwards**

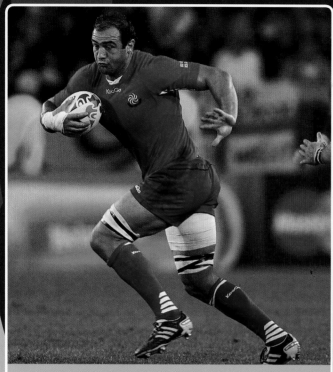

MAMUKA GORGODZE

Country:	Georgia
Club:	Toulon (France)
Position:	Lock, flanker or number 8
Born:	July 14, 1984
Total Caps:	57
Total Points:	115

Skills and strengths: Gorgodze's enormous frame and rampaging runs make him a huge, combative force on the pitch. He is a firm favourite with Georgia fans who have nicknamed him 'Gorgodzilla' because of his powerful hand-off and hunger for confrontation.

Tries and triumphs: With surprising acceleration and huge power, Gorgodze's try record – 23 in total – is the envy of many backs. He is Georgia's leading try scorer.

Claim to fame: Signed for French and European champions Toulon in 2014. Won two man of the match awards at RWC 2011, including one against England despite finishing on the losing side.

ADRIAAN STRAUSS

Country:	South Africa
Club:	Bulls (South Africa)
Position:	Hooker
Born:	November 18, 1985
Total Caps:	44
Total Points:	25

Skills and strengths: A strong scrummager and good lineout thrower, Strauss has excellent ball skills and can surprise opponents with a timely pass or a quick burst of pace and power, taking the ball forward.

Tries and triumphs: Captained the Cheetahs to the Super Rugby playoffs for the first time in 2013 before switching to the Bulls for 2015. Scored his first two tries for the Springboks against Scotland in 2012.

Claim to fame: Engaged in a fierce fight with Bismarck du Plessis for the hooker position in the Springbok team. Strauss won the 2013 South African Super Rugby Player of the Year award.

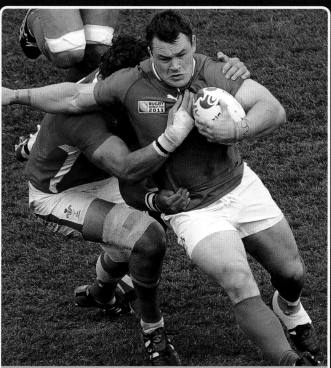

CIAN HEALY

Country:	Ireland
Club:	Leinster (Ireland)
Position:	Prop
Born:	October 7, 1987
Total Caps:	48
Total Points:	15

Skills and strengths: Not just a major force during scrums, the former Clontarf player is very mobile and good at charging down the pitch. Relentless energy and a vast number of tackles in each match make for a highly valued player.

Tries and triumphs: A three-time European champion with wins in 2009, 2011 and 2012. Scored a try against Italy during Ireland's triumphant 2014 Six Nations campaign.

Claim to fame: Man of the match when Ireland defeated Australia at RWC 2011. Healy was selected for the British & Irish Lions 2013 tour but an ankle injury meant he had to withdraw.

ALEX CORBISIERO

Country:	England
Club:	Northampton Saints (England)
Position:	Prop
Born:	August 30, 1988
Total Caps:	21
Total Points:	5

Skills and strengths: Impressive scrummaging technique allied to a powerful frame make this prop a truly fearsome opponent.

Tries and triumphs: A cheeky spin and roll past the Australian defence saw Corbisiero score his first international try in 2013. Part of Northampton Saints' 2013/14 English Premiership-winning season in which he experienced only one defeat.

Claim to fame: Has suffered with injuries but when fit can lay claim to being one of the most accomplished and destructive props in rugby, as witnessed by his part in the dismantling of the Australian scrum in the third British & Irish Lions Test in 2013.

Picture Quiz

WHO'S WHO?

Can you name each of these players? Three have played in a Rugby World Cup Final and the fourth hopes to in 2015.

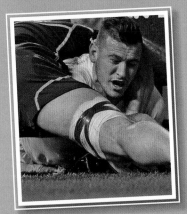

2

3

4

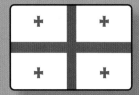

FLAG UP!

Can you match the national flag with these six nations attending Rugby World Cup 2015?

Tonga

Samoa

Georgia

Namibia

Romania

South Africa

1

2

3

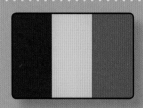

4

5

6

STADIUM MATCH-UP

Can you match the correct name to these images of eight Rugby World Cup 2015 venues?

Twickenham

Sandy Park

Stadium MK

Millennium Stadium

St James' Park

Kingsholm

Manchester City Stadium

Olympic Stadium

1 ....

5 ....

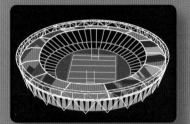

2 ....

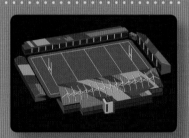

6 ....

3 ....

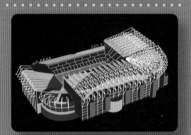

7 ....

4 ....

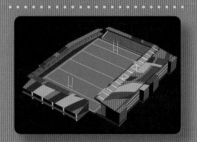

8 ....

ANSWERS:

WHO'S WHO?: 1. Thierry Dusautoir, 2. Danny Care, 3. Bakkies Botha, 4. Richie McCaw

FLAG UP!: 1. Namibia, 2. Samoa, 3. Romania, 4. South Africa, 5. Georgia, 6. Tonga

STADIUM MATCH-UP: 1. Millennium Stadium, 2. Olympic Stadium, 3. Twickenham, 4. Stadium MK, 5. Manchester City Stadium, 6. Sandy Park, 7. St James' Park, 8. Kingsholm

QUIZ 1: 1. Elton Flatley, 2. Romania, 3. Richie McCaw, 4. Japan, 5. Australia, 6. Tonga, 7. Australia, 8. 22, by Australia, 9. Jonah Lomu, 10. Vincent Clerc (11 tries) **QUIZ 2:** 1. Japan, 2. England, 3. Gavin Hastings, 4. Japan, 5. 3, 6. Morné Steyn, 7. Chris Latham, 8. Josh Lewsey, 9. Simon Culhane, 10. Jason Leonard **QUIZ 3:** 1. Argentina, 2. Scotland, 3. South Africa, 4. Japan, 5. France, 6. Ireland, 7. Wales (v France), 8. Scotland (972 pts), 9. Spain, Côte D'Ivoire, 10. USA **QUIZ 4:** 1. Mike Tindall, 2. Gonzalo Quesada (Argentina), 3. Kingsholm, 4. Os Du Randt, 5. Vincent Clerc, 6. Jonny Wilkinson, 7. Frank Bunce, 8. Fiji, 9. John Kirwan, 10. David Codey

Trivia Quiz

So you think you know your rugby and especially Rugby World Cup? Test out your knowledge and memory by tackling these four themed trivia quizzes. The answers are on page 59 but no peeking or you'll be spending time in the sin bin.

QUIZ 1:
MULTI-CHOICE

1. Who scored Rugby World Cup's fastest try against Romania just 18 seconds after kick off: Vincent Clerc, Elton Flatley or Bryan Habana?

2. Which team are nicknamed The Oaks: Georgia, Tonga or Romania?

3. Who captained New Zealand to win the trophy in 2011: Dan Carter, Keven Mealamu or Richie McCaw?

4. Will RWC 2019 be held in Japan, the USA or Australia?

5. Which was the first side to win Rugby World Cup twice: New Zealand, Australia or South Africa?

6. Which country's players have received the most yellow cards (10) and the joint most red cards (3) at Rugby World Cup matches: Argentina, France or Tonga?

7. Did twins Anthony and Saia Faingaa appear at RWC 2011 for Samoa, Australia or Tonga?

8. What's the highest number of tries scored in a Rugby World Cup match: 16, 22 or 29?

9. Was Jonah Lomu, Danny Cipriani or George Gregan the youngest player to appear in a RWC Final?

10. Who is France's leading try scorer at Rugby World Cups: Vincent Clerc, Serge Blanco or Wesley Fofana?

QUIZ 2:
MATCH ACTION

1. Andrew Miller was playing for which team at RWC 2003 when he scored a 52m-long drop goal?

2. Against which team did South Africa's Jannie de Beer strike a record five drop goals in a single match?

3. Is Gavin Hastings, Dan Carter or Jonny Wilkinson Rugby World Cup's leading conversion kicker with 39 successful conversions?

4. Against which team did New Zealand's Marc Ellis score a record six tries in a single RWC match?

5. What is the shirt number of a player starting a match in the tight head prop position?

6. Which South African was the leading points scorer at Rugby World Cup 2011?

7. Is David Pocock, Chris Latham or David Campese Australia's leading try scorer at Rugby World Cups, with 11 tries?

8. Who is the only England player to score five tries in a single RWC match?

9. Did Simon Culhane, Chris Latham or Gavin Hastings notch up 45 points in a single RWC match?

10. Which Englishman has played in 22 Rugby World Cup matches, more than any other player?

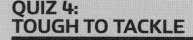

QUIZ 3:
TEAM TALK

1. Which was the only non-European team in England's pool at RWC 2011?

2. Which team scored 13 tries when beating Cote D'Ivoire 89-0 in 1995?

3. Which team has won both RWC Finals they have appeared in without scoring a try?

4. Can you name the first team to concede 1,000 points in Rugby World Cup matches?

5. Which team faced New Zealand in both Rugby World Cup 1987 and the 2011 Final?

6. Which team defeated Australia 15-6 in Pool C of Rugby World Cup 2011?

7. Which team lost their 2011 semi-final by one point despite completing 114 out of their 117 rucks and having 60% possession in the match?

8. Which team has scored the most Rugby World Cup points out of Wales, Scotland and Ireland?

9. Can you name either of the two teams that have played just three matches in Rugby World Cups before the 2015 competition?

10. Takudzwa Ngwenya outsprinted Bryan Habana to score a memorable try at RWC 2007, but for which team was he playing?

QUIZ 4:
TOUGH TO TACKLE

1. In Rugby World Cup 2003 Final, who was the only England player to be substituted before the match went into extra time?

2. Which player has scored the most penalties in a single RWC?

3. Which rugby club ground will host the very last pool match of Rugby World Cup 2015?

4. Which prop is the only non-Australian to play in two Rugby World Cup-winning teams?

5. Sam Warburton received a red card in a RWC 2011 semi-final for a dangerous tackle on which French player?

6. Who is the only player to have scored points in two Rugby World Cup Finals?

7. Which player has played for two different countries, Samoa and New Zealand, at different Rugby World Cups?

8. Which Rugby World Cup-playing country's national flag features a bunch of bananas?

9. Who scored a try from his own 22 versus Italy in the opening match of RWC 1987 and was Italy's head coach during Rugby World Cup 2003?

10. Which Australian forward was sent off after just four minutes of the 1987 third place play-off match versus Wales?

Rugby World Cup 2015 Match Schedule

POOL A

				SCORE
Fri Sept 18	20:00	Twickenham Stadium	England v Fiji	
Sun Sept 20	14:30	Millennium Stadium	Wales v Uruguay	
Wed Sept 23	16:45	Millennium Stadium	Australia v Fiji	
Sat Sept 26	20:00	Twickenham Stadium	England v Wales	
Sun Sept 27	12:00	Villa Park	Australia v Uruguay	
Thurs Oct 1	16:45	Millennium Stadium	Wales v Fiji	
Sat Oct 3	20:00	Twickenham Stadium	England v Australia	
Tues Oct 6	20:00	Stadium MK	Fiji v Uruguay	
Sat Oct 10	16:45	Twickenham Stadium	Australia v Wales	
Sat Oct 10	20:00	Manchester City Stadium	England v Uruguay	

POOL B

				SCORE
Sat Sept 19	16:45	Brighton Community Stadium	South Africa v Japan	
Sun Sept 20	12:00	Brighton Community Stadium	Samoa v USA	
Wed Sept 23	14:30	Kingsholm Stadium	Scotland v Japan	
Sat Sept 26	16:45	Villa Park	South Africa v Samoa	
Sun Sept 27	14:30	Elland Road	Scotland v USA	
Sat Oct 3	14:30	Stadium MK	Samoa v Japan	
Sat Oct 3	16:45	St James' Park	South Africa v Scotland	
Wed Oct 7	16:45	Olympic Stadium	South Africa v USA	
Sat Oct 10	14:30	St James' Park	Samoa v Scotland	
Sun Oct 11	20:00	Kingsholm Stadium	USA v Japan	

POOL C

				SCORE
Sat Sept 19	12:00	Kingsholm Stadium	Tonga v Georgia	
Sun Sept 20	16:45	Wembley Stadium	New Zealand v Argentina	
Thurs Sept 24	20:00	Olympic Stadium	New Zealand v Namibia	
Fri Sept 25	16:45	Kingsholm Stadium	Argentina v Georgia	
Tues Sept 29	16:45	Sandy Park	Tonga v Namibia	
Fri Oct 2	20:00	Millennium Stadium	New Zealand v Georgia	
Sun Oct 4	14:30	Leicester City Stadium	Argentina v Tonga	
Wed Oct 7	20:00	Sandy Park	Namibia v Georgia	
Fri Oct 9	20:00	St James' Park	New Zealand v Tonga	
Sun Oct 11	12:00	Leicester City Stadium	Argentina v Namibia	